Chinese Gr:

Level 1: 30(

秘密花园

Mìmì   Huāyuán

The Secret Garden

Frances Hodgson Burnett

Mind Spark Press LLC

SHANGHAI

Published by Mind Spark Press LLC

Shanghai, China

Mandarin Companion is a trademark of Mind Spark Press LLC.

Copyright © Mind Spark Press LLC , 2013

For information about educational or bulk purchases, please contact
Mind Spark Press at business@mandarincompanion.com.

Instructor and learner resources and traditional Chinese editions of
the Mandarin Companion series are available at
www.MandarinCompanion.com.

First paperback print edition January, 2015

Library of Congress Cataloging-in-Publication Data
Hodgson Burnett, Francis.
The Secret Garden : Mandarin Companion Graded Readers: Level
1, Simplified Chinese Edition / Francis Hodgson Burnett, Renjun
Yang; [edited by] John Pasden, Cui Yu.
1st paperback edition.
Salt Lake City, UT; Shanghai, China: Mind Spark Press LLC, 2014

LCCN: 2014943472

ISNB: 978-1-941875-00-1
ISBN: 978-0-9910052-0-8 (ebook)
ISBN: 978-0-9910052-5-3 (ebook/traditional ch)

All rights reserved; no part of this publication may be reproduced,
stored in a retrieval system, transmitted in any form, or by any means,
electronic, mechanical, photocopying, recording, or otherwise, without the prior written permission of the publishers.

Mandarin Companion Graded Readers

Now you can read books in Chinese that are fun and help accelerate language learning. Every book in the Mandarin Companion series is carefully written to use characters, words, and grammar that a learner is likely to know.

The Mandarin Companion Leveling System has been meticulously developed through an in-depth analysis of textbooks, education programs and natural Chinese language. Every story is written in a simple style that is fun and easy to understand so you improve with each book.

Mandarin Companion Level 1

Level 1 is intended for Chinese learners at an upper-elementary level. Most learners will be able to approach this book after one to two years of formal study, depending on the learner and program. This series is designed to combine simplicity of characters with an easy-to-understand storyline that helps beginner grow their vocabulary and language comprehension abilities. The more they read, the better they will become at reading and grasping the Chinese language.

Level 1 is designed around the Mandarin Companion's core set of 300 basic characters. These basic characters ensure that most of the vocabulary will be simple everyday words that the reader is most likely to know. This series contains approximately 400 unique words; a number low enough to make reading Chinese less intimidating, while also introducing new key words relevant to the story.

Key words are added gradually over the course of the story and a numbered footnote indicates each instance of a key word. Pinyin and an English definition is provided at the bottom of the page for the first instance of each key word and a complete glossary of key words is located at the back of the book. All proper nouns have been underlined to help the reader distinguish between names and key words.

What level is right for me?

If you are able to read this book with a high level of comprehension, then this book is likely at your level. It is ideal to have at most only one unknown word or character for every 40-50 words or characters that are read.

Once you are able to read fluidly and quickly without interruption you are ready for the next level. Even if you are able to understand all of the words in the book, we recommend that readers build fluidity and reading speed before moving to higher levels.

How will this help my Chinese?

Reading extensively in a language you are learning is one of the most effective ways to build fluency. However, the key is to read at a high level of comprehension. Reading at the appropriate level in Chinese will increase the speed of character recognition, help acquire vocabulary faster, allow readers to naturally learn grammar, and train the brain to think in Chinese. It also makes learning Chinese more fun and enjoyable. Readers will experience the sense of accomplishment and confidence that only comes from reading entire books in Chinese.

Extensive Reading

After years of studying Chinese, many people ask, "why can't I become fluent in Chinese?" Fluency can only happen when the language enters our "comfort zone." This comfort comes after significant exposure to and experience with the language. The more times you meet a word, phrase, or grammar point the more readily it will enter your comfort zone.

In the world of language research, experts agree that learners can acquire new vocabulary through reading only if the overall text can be understood. Decades of research indicate that if we know approximately 98% of the words in a book, we can comfortably "pick up" the 2% that is unfamiliar. Reading at this 98% comprehension level is referred to as "extensive reading."

Research in extensive reading has shown that it accelerates vocabulary learning and helps the learner to naturally understand grammar. Perhaps most importantly, it trains the brain to automatically recognize familiar language, thereby freeing up mental energy to focus on meaning and ideas. As they build reading speed and fluency, learners will move from reading "word by word" to processing "chunks of language." A defining feature is that it's less painful than the "intensive reading" commonly used in textbooks. In fact, extensive reading can be downright fun.

Graded Readers

Graded readers are the best books for learners to "extensively" read. Research has taught us that learners need to "encounter" a word 10-30 times before truly learning it, and often many more times for particularly complicated or abstract words. Graded readers are appropriate for learners because the language is controlled and simplified, as opposed to the language in native texts, which is inevitably difficult and often demotivating. Reading extensively with graded readers allows learners to bring together all of the language they have studied and absorb how the words naturally work together.

To become fluent, learners must not only understand the meaning of a word, but also understand its nuances, how to use it in conversation, how to pair it with other words, where it fits into natural word order, and how it is used in grammar structures. No textbook could ever be written to teach all of this explicitly. When used properly, a textbook introduces the language and provides the basic meanings, while graded readers consolidate, strengthen, and deepen understanding.

Without graded readers, learners would have to study dictionaries, textbooks, sample dialogs, and simple conversations until they have randomly encountered enough Chinese for it to enter their comfort zones. With proper use of graded readers, learners can tackle this issue and develop greater fluency now, at their current levels, instead of waiting until some period in the distant future. With a stronger foundation and greater confidence at their current levels, learners are encouraged and motivated to continue their Chinese studies to even greater heights. Plus, they'll quickly learn that reading Chinese is fun!

Table of Contents

Story Adaptation Notes

This story is an adaptation of British author Frances Hodgson Burnett's 1911 classic novel, The Secret Garden. This Mandarin Companion graded reader has been adapted into a fully localized Chinese version of the original story. The characters have been given authentic Chinese names as opposed to transliterations of English names, which sound foreign in Chinese. The locations have been adapted to well-known places in China.

The original story begins in India and later moves to Yorkshire, England when Mary Lennox becomes an orphan. In this adaptation, the locations have been adapted to Hainan and Nanjing, China.

Character Adaptations

The following is a list of the characters from The Secret Garden in Chinese followed by their corresponding English names from the original novel. The names below are not translations; they are new Chinese names used for the Chinese versions of the original characters. Think of them as all-new characters in a Chinese story.

李叶 (Lǐ Yè) - Mary Lennox

马阿姨 (Mǎ Āyí) - Mrs. Medlock

王乐心 (Wáng Lèxīn) - Martha Sowerby

林爷爷 (Lín Yéye) - Ben Weatherstaff

王乐天 (Wáng Lètiān) - Dickon Sowerby

文先生 (Wén Xiānsheng) - Archibald Craven

文思远 (Wén Sīyuǎn) - Colin Craven

文太太 (Wén Tàitai) - Mistress Craven

Cast of Characters

李叶
(Lǐ Yè)

马阿姨
(Mǎ Āyí)

王乐心
(Wáng Lèxīn)

林爷爷
(Lín Yéye)

王乐天
(Wáng Lètiān)

文先生
(Wén Xiānsheng)

文思远
(Wén Sīyuǎn)

文太太
(Wén Tàitai)

Locations

海南 Hǎinán

The southernmost province of China, Hainan is a large tropical island off the southern coast of mainland China. Today it is known as a popular tourist destination for its clear water and white sandy beaches.

南京 Nánjīng

A prominent place in Chinese history and culture, Najing has long been one of China's most important cities. Located in east-central China, it is recognized as one of the Four Great Ancient Capitals of China and today is one of China's largest cities and commercial centers.

— Chapter 1 —
没有人喜欢的女孩

她叫李叶，是一个不太好看的女孩。

李叶出生在海南。海南在中国的最南边，很远很远。李叶的爸爸经常在外面，很少在家。李叶的妈妈是个很好看的女人，她有很多朋友，每天都和朋友一起玩。李叶的爸爸妈妈都很忙，他们没有时间理他们的女儿。还有，李叶的妈妈好像一点也不喜欢李叶，她觉得李叶一点也不像她。李叶出生以后，她就告诉家里的阿姨："如果你们想让我开心，就不要让我看到这个孩子。"

---

1 玩 (wán) *v.* to play
2 理 (lǐ) *v.* to pay attention to
3 好像 (hǎoxiàng) *v.* it seems
4 阿姨 (āyí) *n.* maid, housekeeper
5 开心 (kāixīn) *adj.* happy

所以，李叶很少能见到她的爸爸妈妈。

李叶真的跟她的妈妈不一样，她看起来又瘦又小，还经常生病。她总是喜欢生气，生气的时候总是哭。如果李叶的妈妈听到她哭，就会很生气。所有的人都不喜欢这个孩子，他们从来没有见过这样的孩子。为了不让李叶哭，她的阿姨总是很听李叶的话。李叶喜欢什么，她的阿姨就给她什么。李叶觉得在这个家里只有她的阿姨关心她。

李叶还不到十岁的时候，有一天，她早上起来以后看到一个新的阿姨，又

6 看起来 (kànqǐlai) *vc.* to look
   (a certain way)
7 瘦 (shòu) *adj.* thin
8 生病 (shēngbìng) *v.* to get sick
9 总是 (zǒngshì) *adv.* always
10 生气 (shēngqì) *vo.* to get angry

11 哭 (kū) *v.* to cry
12 为了 (wèile) *conj.* for the purpose
   of, in order to
13 听话 (tīnghuà) *vo.* to obey, *lit.*
   "to listen to (someone's) words"
14 关心 (guānxīn) *v.* to be concerned
   about

生气了，因为她想要以前的阿姨。阿姨
告诉李叶：“她不会来了。”李叶更生气
了，她让这个新阿姨马上出去，让以前
的阿姨马上来。可是很长时间，她的新

阿姨没有回来，她以前的阿姨也没来。

那一天和平时不一样，没有人跟她说话，也没有人跟她玩。她很不开心，不知道为什么今天只有她一个人。一定出事了！

后来，她听到妈妈和别人说话，才知道真的出事了。她家里很多人都生病了，不到两天就死了很多人。李叶很难过，因为所有人都不理她。她一个人回到房间哭了一会儿，然后睡了很久。她起来的时候，还是没有人来看她。

"这儿有个孩子！"后来，几个人发现了又瘦又小的李叶，她一个人在房间里。

---

15 平时 (píngshí) *tn.* usual; usually

16 一定 (yídìng) *adv.* definitely

17 出事 (chūshì) *vo.* to have an accident

18 后来 (hòulái) *tn.* afterwards

19 难过 (nánguò) *adj.* to feel upset

20 发现 (fāxiàn) *v.* to discover

"孩子，你是谁？为什么在这里？"有个人问她。

"我叫李叶，我睡了很久。为什么我的阿姨不来？"李叶问。

"孩子，他们都死了。"

后来李叶才知道，她的爸爸妈妈和以前的阿姨都死了，别人都走了。没有人想到这个孩子，因为他们不喜欢她，所以没有人关心她。

— Chapter 2 —

去南京

李叶的爸爸妈妈死了以后，她在海南没有别的家人了，但是她有一个叔叔在南京。
₂₁
₂₂

他的叔叔是一个很有钱的人。知道李叶的事以后，叔叔让家里的阿姨带李叶来南京。
₂₂
₂₂
_{4 23}

叔叔家的阿姨姓马，是一个又高又瘦的女人。李叶很不喜欢她，也不理她。
₂₂
₄
₇
₂

马阿姨好像也不喜欢李叶。她觉得孩子应该可爱听话，可是李叶又瘦
₃
₂₄
₁₃
₇

---

21 家人 (jiārén) *n.* family

22 叔叔 (shūshu) *n.* uncle, father's younger brother

23 带 (dài) *v.* to bring

24 应该 (yīnggāi) *aux.* should, ought to

又小，总是不理别人，她从来没有见过这么不可爱的孩子。

但是马阿姨很喜欢说话，看到李叶不理她，她就问："你认识你的叔叔吗？"

"不认识。"李叶说。

"你的爸爸妈妈没有跟你说过他吗？"马阿姨又问。

"没有。"想到爸爸妈妈很少跟她说话，李叶更不开心了。

"你知不知道你要去一个很奇怪的地方？"马阿姨问。李叶不说话。马阿姨觉得这个孩子真奇怪，一点也不关心她要去哪儿。

看见李叶不说话，马阿姨又说：

25 奇怪 (qíguài) *adj.* weird, strange

"文先生的房子很老，已经六百年了。房子里有一百个房间，房间里面的东西都很贵。但是很多房间都关着，我们都不可以进去。房子外面有几个很大的花园，有很多树。"

李叶觉得叔叔的家很有意思，跟海南很不一样。但是她不想让马阿姨知道她的想法，所以还是不说话。

"你觉得怎么样？"马阿姨问。

"我没有想法。"李叶说。

"你跟文先生一样奇怪。我不知道你为什么要去南京，但是我知道文先生一定不会跟你说话，因为他从来不关心别人。文先生的身体有病，认识他的

---

26 里面 (lǐmiàn) *n.* inside
27 有意思 (yǒuyìsi) *adj.* interesting
28 想法 (xiǎngfǎ) *n.* thinking, idea

太太以前，他从来没有开心过。"马阿姨
说。

　　李叶没想到这个奇怪的叔叔有
太太，马阿姨觉得李叶很想听，又说：
"他的太太是一个很好看的女人，文先生
很爱他的太太，她死的时候……"

　　"什么？她死了？" 李叶觉得很
奇怪，马上问。

　　"对。太太死了以后，文先生又
像以前一样奇怪了。他在家的时候，
总是在房间里，不想见人，只有很少的
人可以看到他。你也别想看到他，你
只能自己玩。"马阿姨说。

　　李叶坐在车上，想了很久：叔叔家

有很大的花园，花园里有很多树，很多花；还有一百个房间，但是不可以进去；叔叔是一个奇怪的人……她在南京会怎么样，她也不知道。

— Chapter 3 —
这个阿姨不一样

两天以后，李叶和马阿姨到了叔叔家。

李叶觉得这是一个很奇怪的地方。叔叔的房子很大，有很多房间，但是为什么很多房间的门都关着？外面有很大的花园和草地，但是为什么看不到人？李叶很不喜欢这个地方。想到以后要住在这里，她有点生气，又想哭了。

马阿姨带李叶走了很久，最后，她们走进了一个又大又黑的房间。马阿姨对李叶说："我们到了。这就是

---
29 草地 (cǎodì) *n.* lawn, grassy area

你的房间。文先生现在不想见你，如果他想见你，我会来告诉你。记住，你只可以在这个房间里玩，不可以去别的房间。"然后，马阿姨走了。

很快，天黑了。李叶一个人在这个又大又黑的房间里，觉得很难过。她哭了一会儿，然后就睡了。

第二天早上，李叶看到一个新的阿姨在房间里。她不想理这个阿姨，但是新阿姨对李叶说："你好，我叫王乐心。你喜欢这里吗？"

"不喜欢。很不喜欢！"李叶说。

"那是因为你刚来这里。如果你住久一点，你就会喜欢这里。"王乐心

---

30 记住 (jìzhu) *vc.* to remember, to memorize

说，"我很喜欢这里。你看，那边有一块

大草地，有很多花，很多树，还有很多
₂₉
小鸟。天气好的时候，小鸟会来跟你

说话。"

李叶觉得这个阿姨很奇怪，她跟海南的阿姨不一样。在海南，阿姨从来不跟李叶说很多话。李叶跟她们说话的时候，她们才跟李叶说话。她们总是很听李叶的话。李叶让她们做什么，她们就做什么。

李叶看了一下王乐心，她穿着黄衣服，又黑又瘦，但是看起来很健康也很快乐。

"你是我的新阿姨吗？"李叶问。

"我会帮你做一些事，但是我不会一直在你身边。"王乐心说。

"那谁给我穿衣服？"李叶问。

"什么？你不会穿衣服吗？"王乐心问。

---

31 衣服 (yīfu) *n.* clothing
32 健康 (jiànkāng) *adj.* healthy
33 一直 (yīzhí) *adv.* all along

"不会。我从来没有自己穿过衣服。"李叶说。

"我从来没有见过你这样的孩子。你现在应该学会自己穿衣服。"王乐心说。

听到阿姨这样对她说话，李叶很生气，又哭了。她从来没有见过这样的阿姨，她不喜欢这个阿姨。

看到李叶哭了，王乐心笑了，说："好了，好了，别哭了。快起来吧，我帮你穿衣服。"她一边帮李叶穿衣服，一边对她说自己的家人："我们家有12个人。爸爸妈妈没有时间理我们，我们10个孩子就在大草地里玩。妈妈说外面的好天气可以让我们更健康，所以我们家的孩子都像快乐健康的小马。我的弟弟王乐天今年12岁，他有一只小马，又黑又可爱。"

"他在哪里找到那只小马的？"李叶也想有一只小马。

"他在大草地里找到的。那只小马是他的好朋友，每天都跟他一起玩。我弟弟是个好男孩，小鸟和小马都喜欢他。"王乐心开心地说。

李叶觉得王乐天很有意思。这是她第一次觉得别人有意思。

中午，王乐心给李叶做了很多好吃的东西。但是李叶觉得不饿，不想吃东西。王乐心说："如果我的弟弟妹妹

在这里，他们一定很快就吃完了。他们
经常觉得饿，从来没有吃过这么多好吃
的东西。"

"我从来没有饿过。所以我不知道什么是饿。"李叶说。

"今天天气很好，如果你不想吃东西，就去花园里玩一会儿吧。"王乐心说。

"谁跟我一起去？"李叶问。

"我没有时间，你应该自己去。王乐天就是一个人去大草地里玩的。"王乐心说。听到王乐天的名字，李叶一下子很想去花园走一走。

王乐心说："你出门以后，一直往前走，就可以走到花园。那里还有一个小花园，十年了，从来没有人进去过。"

35 往前 (wǎngqián) *phr.* forward

"为什么？"李叶觉得很奇怪，马上问。

"十年前，文先生的太太死了。后来他就关了花园，不让别人进去，他自己也不进去。没有人知道门在哪里。我要走了，马阿姨在叫我。"

— Chapter 4 —
有人在哭

王乐心走了以后，李叶一直在想那
个小花园。十年了，从来没有人进过那
个花园。它现在是什么样子？她很想看
一看。叔叔为什么不让别人进去？他那
么爱他的太太，为什么不喜欢他太太的
花园？

李叶想了很久，最后来到花园里，
想找到王乐心说的那个地方。但是找了
很久，她都没有找到那个小花园。

就在李叶想回去的时候，她发现
了一只小鸟。那只鸟的头小小的，身体

36 样子 (yàngzi) *n.* appearance

是黑色和黄色的，很可爱。那只小鸟一边飞，一边快乐地叫，好像在对李叶说："你好，我们一起玩吧。"

小鸟飞的时候，李叶就在它后面跑。跑到一个果园的时候，李叶看到一个老人。那个老人在种树。他看起来不怎么开心，看到李叶以后没有理她。

"这是什么地方？"李叶问他。

"一个果园。"老人说。

"那边是什么地方？"李叶又问。

"一个菜园。"老人又说。

就在他们说话的时候，那只小鸟又飞过来了。老人看到小鸟，一下子就笑了。他对小鸟说："孩子，你飞去

37 种 (zhòng) *v.* to plant (a tree or other plant) 38 不怎么 (bùzěnme) *adv.* not very

哪儿了？我今天一直没看到你。”

李叶问老人：“你认识这只鸟吗？”

老人说：“我们是朋友。它刚出生的时候，鸟妈妈就死了，它没有家人。”

李叶听到老人这样说，也很难过。
她说："我跟它一样，也是一个人。"

"你就是从海南来的那个女孩吗？"
老人问李叶。

"是的。你叫什么名字？"李叶问
老人。

"我姓林，你叫我林爷爷吧。我在
文先生的花园里做事，已经在这里40
多年了。我也是一个人，没有别的朋
友。"

就在这个时候，小鸟飞走了，飞到
了很高的树上，树在一面墙后面。李叶
问林爷爷："那面墙后面是一个花园吗？
那是我叔叔的太太的花园吗？我很想

---

39 做事 (zuòshì) *vo.* to do things　　40 墙 (qiáng) *n.* wall

进去，可是听说没有门。"

"那个花园十年以前有门，可是现在没有了。"听到花园，林爷爷好像不高兴了，说："你走吧，我要做事了。"

后来，李叶经常跑去花园，去那儿和小鸟玩。她还想找到那个小花园的门。

有一天吃饭的时候，她一下子吃完了所有的东西。王乐心笑了，对她说："你现在的样子看起来比以前健康了。以前你又黄又瘦，像黄色的树叶。我妈妈说得对，外面的好天气会让人很健康。"

李叶一直在想那个小花园的事，她

问王乐心："我叔叔为什么不喜欢那个花园？为什么他关了花园，也不让别人找到花园的门？"

王乐心说："我知道你一直没有忘记那个花园。马阿姨不让我们说花园的事，所以你记住，我告诉你以后，你一定不要告诉别人。"李叶说："我一定不会告诉别人。"然后王乐心就说："文太太很喜欢那个花园，她和文先生一起打理，从来不让别人进去。文太太很喜欢坐在花园里的树上。有一天，文太太从树上掉了下来，第二天就死了。文先生很难过，从那以后，他再也没进去过，也不让别人

---

41 忘记 (wàngjì) v. to forget   43 掉 (diào) v. to fall

42 打理 (dǎlǐ) v. to take care of

进去。我听说花园在一面很高的墙

后面，但是没有人知道门在哪里。"

就在这个时候，李叶听到了一个

孩子的哭声，好像很远又好像很近。
她问王乐心："我好像听到有人在哭！你
听到了吗？"王乐心一下子很紧张，马上
关了门，说："我没有听到，你一定听错
了，那是外面的风，没有人哭。"后来，
李叶又听到了关门声，然后，哭声就
没有了。王乐心又说："你听，是风关了
门。"但是，看到王乐心紧张的样子，
李叶觉得她没有说真话。

---

44 声 (shēng) *n.* noise, sound   45 紧张 (jǐnzhāng) *adj.* nervous

— Chapter 5 —
秘密花园

第二天上午，天气很不好，外面的风很大。李叶又想去花园，可是王乐心对她说："你现在很喜欢出去，这很好。可是今天风太大了，有点冷，如果你出去，会生病的。"

李叶问："那我今天做什么？"

"你为什么不看书？"王乐心说。

"我没有书。"李叶说。

"文先生的书房里有很多书，你可以去那里看书。但是你要先问问马阿姨。"王乐心说完就走了。

李叶没有问王乐心书房在哪里，也不想去问马阿姨，她想自己找到它。李叶想："如果我找不到书房，那也没关系。我更想知道，别的房间里有什么东西。"李叶记得她刚来这里的时候，马阿姨就告诉她，叔叔的房子里有很多房间，但是很多房间都关着，她也不可以去别的房间。所以，她现在很想进几个房间看看。

那天上午，李叶走了很远，她想去远一点的房间看看。她到了一个房间前面，试了一下，打开了门，走了进去。李叶发现那是一个很大的房间，房间里有很多有意思的东西。后来，

---

46 记得 (jìde) *v.* to remember   48 打开 (dǎkāi) *vc.* to open
47 试 (shì) *v.* to try

李叶 打开了更多的房间。她在那些房间
里玩了很久。

　　中午的时候，李叶饿了，她想回
自己的房间吃饭。可是，李叶 发现她
不知道怎么回去了。她找了很久，还是
找不到自己的房间。就在这个时候，她
又听到了那个孩子的哭 声。

　　"这次的哭 声比昨晚近了一些。"
李叶一边想一边往哭 声的方向走，她
觉得哭 声更近了，好像就在前面的那个
房间里。她想开门，可是，马阿姨
一下子出来了。她看起来很生气，
大声说："你来这里做什么？我告诉过
你，你只能在你的房间里玩。快回去。"

49 方向 (fāngxiàng) *n.* direction

"可是我听到有人在哭。"李叶说。

"没有人在哭，你一定听错了。
快回去，不然我打你。"马阿姨 生气地

带 李叶回到自己的房间。

马阿姨走了以后，李叶也很生气。她知道她没有听错，真的有人在哭。

下午，外面的天气好了很多，李叶去了花园。到了花园里，李叶觉得开心多了。她看到林爷爷和那只小鸟也在花园里。她跑过去，对小鸟说："你还记得我吗？"

"记得。它怎么会不记得你？它知道这花园里所有的事。"林爷爷说。

"如果你记得我，那你能告诉我那面墙 里面是一个花园吗？"李叶大声问小鸟。

这时候，小鸟一边往前飞一边叫。

李叶笑了，也往前跑。跑到一个树林里，小鸟飞到树上，一直对李叶叫，好像在对李叶说话。李叶高兴地说："你想让我上去吗？"李叶想上去和小鸟玩，可是不小心，她掉了下来。就在这个时候，她发现草地上有一个小东西，很亮，很好看。李叶发现这是一个钥匙，高兴地想："钥匙！这就是秘密花园的钥匙吗？如果是，如果我能找到秘密花园的门，我就可以进去了。可是，门在哪里？"

李叶对小鸟说："小鸟，谢谢你帮我找到了钥匙。你一定知道花园的门在哪里，快告诉我吧。"就在这个时候，

---

51 树林 (shùlín) *n.* forest
52 小心 (xiǎoxīn) *v.* to be careful
53 亮 (liàng) *adj.* bright
54 钥匙 (yàoshi) *n.* key
55 秘密 (mìmì) *n.* secret

树林里有了很大的风，李叶看到墙边的
一些树一直在动。她好像看到了一个
黑色的东西，她走过去看了一下，高兴
地说："是门，是秘密花园的门！"

她用钥匙小心地打开门，走进去，
然后关上了门。

这个花园很奇怪，外面是墙，里面
有很多花、草和树，可是它们好像都

56 关上 (guānshang) vc. to close

死了。"这里以前一定很好看。" 李叶小声说，"已经十年了，这十年里，我是第一个进花园的人。"

李叶在花园里看了很久，发现这里还有一些绿色的草和叶子，她一下子很开心："这里的花和草没有死。我要让这个花园像以前一样好看！"

— Chapter 6 —
两个人的秘密

天黑以后，李叶才从花园出来。她今天很开心，因为她找到了秘密花园，这是她的秘密。

"我明天还要来。"李叶对自己说。

回到房间以后，李叶很饿，吃了很多东西。她一边吃饭一边问王乐心怎么种花、种草。她问的时候很小心，不想让王乐心发现她的秘密。

"我想要一些种花的工具。"李叶说。

"你要用这些工具做什么？"王乐心问她。

---

57 工具 (gōngjù) *n.* tool

"我想要一个自己的花园，种一些花、草和树。"李叶说。

"你说得对，你应该有一个自己的小花园，我觉得它会让你开心的。"王乐心说，"可是，你没有地，你应该让文先生给你一块地。"

"那你能帮我买那些工具吗？"李叶问。

"没问题，我可以让我弟弟王乐天帮你买。花、草、树这些事，他什么都懂。他买了这些工具以后，我让他送来。"王乐心开心地说。

"真的吗？我可以见到王乐天了，我一直很想见他。"李叶高兴地说。

58 问题 (wèntí) *n.* problem

两天以后，李叶很早就去了花园，因为今天王乐天会在花园等她，给她送种花的工具。

到了花园以后，李叶看到一个男孩，他身边还有很多小鸟和一只小马，他在学小鸟的叫声。他看到李叶以后，开心地笑了，说："你是李叶吧？我是王乐天。这是你要的种花的工具和种子。"王乐天很瘦，可是很好看。

"对，我是李叶。谢谢你。你为什么学小鸟的叫声？"李叶问。

"因为我们是朋友，我刚刚在和它们说话。"王乐天说。

李叶觉得很有意思，王乐天能听懂

59 种子 (zhǒngzi) *n.* seed

小鸟说话，小鸟也能听懂王乐天说话。

"你能给我看一下种子吗？"李叶问。

"好。这些种子的花是黄色的，

那些是红色的。这里还有一些工具，你可以种花、种草。"然后他又告诉李叶怎么种花和种草。最后，他对李叶说："告诉我你的花园在哪里，我们可以一起种花。"

李叶一下子很不好意思，她不知道要不要告诉他。但是她觉得王乐天是个好人，他能让秘密花园像以前一样好看。她觉得应该告诉王乐天自己的秘密。过了一会儿，她说："我告诉你一个秘密，但是你不可以告诉别人。"

王乐天马上说："没问题。我一定不告诉别人。我从来没有告诉别人这些小鸟的家在哪里。"

"我找到了我叔叔的秘密花园，找到了钥匙，我还找到了花园的门。我想打理那个花园，让它像以前一样好看。你能帮我吗？"李叶小声说。

"真的吗？我以前听说过那个花园，我也很想去。它在哪儿？"王乐天很高兴。

"跟我来。"李叶说。然后，她带王乐天去了那个秘密花园。

王乐天在花园里看了很久，然后说："这个地方很好看。但是它好像睡了很久。"他在花园里走了一会儿，又说："这里的花、树和草没有都死。

你看，这里还有一些绿色。我们可以让它像以前一样好看。”

那天，李叶和王乐天 一直在打理秘密花园，天黑了才出来。最后，王乐天说：“以后我每天都会来这里帮你。”

“你不会告诉别人，是不是？”李叶问。

“放心吧，不会的。这个花园是我们两个人的秘密。”王乐天笑了，李叶知道他说的是真话。

60 放心 (fàngxīn) *v.* to relax, to be relieved

— Chapter 7 —

是他在哭！

那天晚上，外面的风声很大，李叶没办法 睡觉，她觉得这风声听起来像哭声。一下子，风声没有了，李叶真的听到了哭声。李叶觉得很奇怪，为什么总是有哭声？这哭声是从哪儿来的？她要再去看一看。

太晚了，所有的人都睡了，外面只有李叶一个人。"上次，我是在一个房间的外面看到马阿姨的，她那么生气，哭声 一定就在那个房间里。"李叶想。她很快找到了那个房间。

---

61 办法 (bànfǎ) *n.* way, method　62 睡觉 (shuìjiào) *vo.* to sleep

"没错，真的有人在房间里哭。"

李叶马上打开门，走了进去。她发现这个房间很大，里面的家具很新，有一张大床，上面有一个男孩。"是他在哭！"李叶太紧张了，不知道应该说什么，只是看着这个男孩。他看起来10岁左右，身体很瘦，一点儿也不健康，好像病了很久。

"你是谁？"男孩不哭了，好像也很紧张。

"你是谁？"李叶也问他。

"我是文思远。"男孩说。

"我是李叶，文先生是我的叔叔。我的爸爸妈妈都死了，所以我从海南

---

63 家具 (jiājù) *n.* furniture

64 左右 (zuǒyòu) *adv.* about, more or less, *lit.* "left-right"

来到这里。"李叶说。

"文先生是我爸爸。"男孩又说。

"叔叔有一个儿子！"李叶觉得很奇怪，"为什么阿姨和叔叔都没告诉过我？我也从来没见过你？"

"我不想让别人看见我，也不想让别人说到我。"男孩说。

"为什么？"李叶问。

"因为我身体不好，总是生病。我快死了。"男孩一下子又哭了。

"这里真的很奇怪，总是有那么多秘密。"李叶想。然后她又问男孩："你爸爸常常来看你吗？"

"不，他很少来。马阿姨说他又

去旅行了。我妈妈在我出生的时候就死了，他见到我的时候总是想到我妈妈，所以他恨我，不想见到我。"男孩难过地说。

"因为你妈妈死了，所以你爸爸也恨那个秘密花园？"李叶问。

"什么秘密花园？"男孩问。

"那是你妈妈喜欢的花园。你妈妈死了以后，叔叔就关了花园。十年了，没有人进去过，也没有人知道钥匙和花园的门在哪里。"李叶说。

"我可以让阿姨找花园的钥匙，让她们带我去花园。"

李叶一下子很紧张，她觉得自己不

应该告诉文思远 秘密花园的事。如果文思远告诉了别人，她和王乐天就没有秘密了。所以李叶说："如果你让别人带你去花园，那个花园就不是秘密了。"

"秘密？什么意思？"文思远问。

"你想想，如果我们能找到秘密花园，它就是我们自己的花园。我们可以进去玩，没有人知道我们在哪里。多有意思，对不对？"李叶说。

文思远一下子懂了，他说："我从来不知道什么是秘密，可是我觉得有秘密会很不错。"

李叶又说："我们可以一起去秘密花园，你的病很快就会好的。"

文思远一下子笑了，高兴地说："我很想去那个秘密花园。以后你要经常来这里。如果你不来，我就让王乐心去找你。"

李叶也笑了，她知道为什么王乐心听到哭声的时候那么紧张了。李叶说："好，我明天再来。记住，那个花园是我们的秘密，不要告诉别人。"说完，李叶就回自己的房间了。

— Chapter 8 —
三个人的秘密

第二天天气很好，李叶很早就起床了，她想先去秘密花园，因为王乐天在那里等她，他们要一起打理花园。然后，她要去看一看文思远。

那天，李叶和王乐天在秘密花园里做了很多事。他们种了很多红色和黄色的花、绿色的草，还种了很多树，花园比以前好看了。

从花园出来以后，李叶马上就去看文思远了。文思远给李叶看他的书，李叶告诉文思远很多海南的事，他们在

68 起床 (qǐchuáng) *vo.* to get out of bed

一起笑，很快乐。

文思远的阿姨觉得很奇怪。这个

男孩从来不笑，只会哭，但是他看到
李叶以后，快乐了很多。

"我觉得你应该见见王乐天，他跟你
太不一样了。"李叶说。

"王乐天是谁？"文思远问。

李叶很喜欢说王乐天："他是
王乐心的弟弟，今年12岁。他会和小鸟
说话，每天都去大草地，他知道小鸟
住在什么地方。"

"我什么都没见过，因为我有病。
我不能去大草地，也不能去花园。"
文思远难过地说。

"为什么不能？可能很快你就可以
去。"李叶说。

69 可能 (kěnéng) *adv.* possibly, maybe

"不，我不能，我要死了。别人都这么说。"文思远说。

"你不会死。只要你每天出门，外面的好天气就会让你的身体很健康。"李叶说。

有一天，李叶很晚才从花园回来。王乐心很紧张地说："你知道文思远的事了，对吗？他现在很生气，因为你没有去看他。他已经哭了很久了。马阿姨也不知道应该怎么办，你快去看看吧。"

文思远看到李叶以后，生气地问："你今天为什么没来？"

"因为我和王乐天有很多事要做。"李叶说。

文思远更生气了，大声说："以后我不让他再去我的花园。"

李叶也生气了，她也大声说："如果你不让他去花园，我就再也不来看你了。"

文思远又哭了，哭声很大。马阿姨和王乐心更紧张了，王乐心对李叶说："请你让他别哭了。如果他再哭，他又会生病的。"

李叶看看文思远，他一直睡在床上，每天都在等自己跟他说话，李叶也觉得有点难过。她走过去，小声对文思远说："别哭了！如果你不哭，我就告诉你秘密花园的事。"听到秘密花园，文思远一下子不哭了，马上问："你找到钥匙了？"

李叶说："对，我找到了花园的门和钥匙。你现在睡觉吧，我明天和王乐天一起带你去秘密花园。"文思远笑了，很快就睡了。

Chapter 9
一起去花园

因为第二天要去秘密花园，所以文思远很早就起床了。

为了不让别人知道他们的秘密，文思远对马阿姨说："今天我要去花园里走走。但是我不想看到别人。我去的时候，所有人都不可以在花园里。我回来以后，他们才可以进花园。"

马阿姨听到文思远这样说，觉得很奇怪。因为文思远很少出门，也不喜欢出门。马阿姨说："我以为你不喜欢出门。"

"如果就我一个人，我一定不想

出去，但是这次李叶会和我一起去。"
文思远说。

"我跟你们一起去吧？外面有点
冷，如果你不小心，你会生病的。"
马阿姨紧张地说。

"我不要你去。跟李叶在一起，我就
会好很多。王乐天也会和我们一起去，
没问题。"文思远说。

听到王乐天的名字，马阿姨就
放心了。因为知道大草地的人都知道
王乐天。大家都觉得王乐天是一个又
健康又喜欢帮别人的人。"如果王乐天
可以帮你，那我就放心了。他是这里
最好的男孩。"马阿姨说。

过了一会儿，王乐天和李叶就来了。因为文思远身体一直不好，总是睡在床上，很少下床走路，所以他很难走到花园。

王乐天找到了一个轮椅，他们要用

70 走路 (zǒulù) *vo.* to walk　　71 轮椅 (lúnyǐ) *n.* wheelchair

这个轮椅帮文思远去花园。

出门以后，文思远很高兴。他坐在轮椅上，一会儿看看天，一会儿看看树，他从来没有觉得花园这么好看。"你听，是鸟的叫声吗？我很久没出门了，快忘了鸟的叫声了。"文思远问李叶。

"是的。是小鸟，它们在跟你说话。今天你能来花园，它们很高兴。"李叶高兴地说。

因为文思远不让别人去花园，所以这个时候，花园里没有别人。但是他们不想让别人发现他们的秘密，所以先在大花园里玩了一会儿。

"到了。"李叶又紧张又高兴地说，"这就是秘密花园的门。"

"是这里！快，我要进去。"文思远高兴地大声说。他们小心地进了花园，然后关了门。

— Chapter 10 —
你可以做到!

文思远坐在轮椅上，认真地看了
一下秘密花园，就像李叶和王乐天
第一次来这里的时候一样。这次，秘密
花园好像比以前好看了，很多黄色和
红色的花都开了，绿草也从地下出
来了，树比以前高了。为了这个男孩，
花园可能也想让自己更好看。

"我真不知道应该说些什么！我快11
岁了，十一年有很多天，但是今天是我
最快乐的一天！"文思远小声说。

"是的。我觉得这一定是最好的

---

72 认真 (rènzhēn) *adj.* serious, earnest

一天。"王乐天说。

"那里还有树！可是看起来有点奇怪。"文思远对李叶说。

李叶知道，文思远的妈妈就是从树上掉下来的。她不想让文思远难过，就说："它很老了。但是几个月以后，所有的花和叶子就会长出来。到时候，它就是最好看的树。"

后来，文思远就坐在轮椅上，看李叶和王乐天打理花园。他又快乐又难过，说："我真喜欢这里！以后我每天都要来。可是，如果我能像你们一样，可以走，可以种花、种草就好了。"

"你会的。你马上就会很健康。

你会跟我们一样，每天走路来花园！"

李叶说。

"走路？我行吗？"文思远问。

"一定行！"李叶马上说。

就在这个时候，他们听到有人很

生气地说："你们怎么进去的？快出来！"

他们往上看，发现 林爷爷就在墙外面，很生气地看着他们。

李叶一下子不知道应该怎么办，她紧张地说："林爷爷，是小鸟帮我找到这个花园的。"

这是第一次别人对文思远这样说话。他坐在轮椅上，也很生气。他问林爷爷："你知道我是谁吗？"

林爷爷认真地看了一下文思远，好像一下子想到了什么，说："是你！你跟你妈妈长得一样！你就是那个小病人！"

"我不是病人！不是！"文思远更生气了。

"他不是。"李叶也生气了，大声说。

"如果你没生病，怎么一直坐在轮椅上？你怎么不起来？你如果真的没生病，就走过来。过来！"林爷爷说。

"文思远，你能做到，你一定能做到。你起来！"李叶说。

"看着我！"文思远大声说。他一下子从轮椅上起来了，小心地走，走了很久，最后，他走到了墙边。文思远哭了，然后高兴地说："你们看，我没有病，我做到了！"李叶和王乐天也高兴地哭了。

— Chapter 11 —

在花园里!

文思远不想让别人知道他们的秘密，所以他让李叶带林爷爷进了秘密花园。他告诉林爷爷："以前，这里是我妈妈的花园。现在它是我的花园了，我喜欢这里。可是这是一个秘密，你不能告诉别人，只有我、李叶、王乐天和你知道。"

林爷爷说："你妈妈很喜欢这个花园，她经常让我帮他打理。你妈妈死了以后，你爸爸关了这个花园。可是我也不想让这个花园死。所以，你们放心吧，这也是我的秘密，我不会告诉别人。"

那天下午，从花园回房间以后，文思远觉得很饿，他吃了很多东西。马阿姨觉得有点奇怪，对文思远说："你今天在外面太久了。你觉得身体怎么样？"

"没问题，我觉得好多了。明天我还要去花园。"文思远说。

后来，天气好的时候，文思远每天都去花园。他每天都在花园里走一走，看看花、草和树，和小鸟一起玩。有时候，他还帮李叶和王乐天打理花园。回房间以后，他总是觉得很饿，吃很多东西。

李叶高兴地发现，文思远的身体健康了很多，也很少生气了。阿姨们看到文思远跟以前很不一样，都觉得很奇怪。

有一天，在花园里，文思远坐在轮椅上，对李叶和王乐天说："我不会告诉别人我的身体健康多了，这是我最大的秘密。我每天都要坐轮椅来这里。我爸爸回来以后，我会自己走到他的房间，对他说'我来了，我的身体很健康，是花园帮了我。以后，我要做一个有用的男人！'"

在花园里，文思远和李叶都学会

73 有用 (yǒuyòng) *adj.* useful

了很多。他们学会了不该只想到自己。现在，他们常常想到花园、王乐天和小鸟。他们比以前更可爱了。

就在文思远的身体一点点健康的时候，文先生还在北京旅行。他去了很多地方，但是没有太太，他在每个地方都不开心。

有一天，文先生在一个花园里睡觉的时候，好像看到了他的太太。

"你在哪儿？我好想你！"文先生问。

"在花园里！在花园里！"文太太一直说。

文先生回到房间以后，有人告诉他家里出了大事，让他马上回家。

— Chapter 12 —
没有秘密了

几天以后，文先生回到了南京。刚到家，马阿姨就跑过来告诉他："先生，思远他……"

文先生一下子很紧张，问："他怎么了？"

"他和以前不一样了。"马阿姨又说。

"他现在在哪里？"文先生不太紧张了。

"在花园里。"马阿姨说。

"在花园里！"文先生大声说。

他马上去了花园。可是他已经十年没来这里了，也忘了钥匙在哪里。他不知道为什么太太让他来这里。这个时候，他听到了花园里孩子的笑声。

　　"有人在里面！"文先生想，"太奇怪了。十年了，没有人进过这个花园！他们怎么会有这个花园的钥匙呢？我要进去看看。"

　　文先生刚要开门，一个孩子很快地跑了出来。但是看到文先生，这个孩子马上不跑了。文先生看了看这个男孩子，高高的，瘦瘦的，看起来很健康。

　　"爸爸！"这个男孩子叫他。

"你是……思远吗？"文先生问。

"是我，爸爸，我是思远！你不认识我了吗？"文思远从来没有想过他会跟爸爸这样见面，但是现在见到爸爸，他还是很高兴。他都快哭了。

文先生一下子不知道说什么，只是小声说："在花园里！在花园里！"

"是的。"文思远说，"因为这个花园，我好多了。但是阿姨们都不知道我好了，这是个秘密，因为我想让你第一个知道。"

文先生哭了，他高兴地哭了。他对文思远说："我以为这个花园已经死了！"

"以前李叶也这么想，"文思远说，

"但是，它现在好了。它跟以前一样好看了。"

后来，他们进了花园，跟李叶和王乐天一起坐在树下。文先生告诉了他们很多花园和文太太的事。文先生第一次觉得关了这个花园是错的；

第一次觉得这个花园没有死；第一次觉得和思远在一起也可以很快乐。文先生和思远一样，觉得在很长很长的时间里他们从来没有这么快乐过。最后，文思远说："这再也不是秘密花园了，我再也不要坐轮椅了。爸爸，我们一起走回去吧。"

马阿姨和王乐心看到文先生和一个健康快乐的男孩子一起走回来的时候，她们觉得很奇怪，但是又很高兴。因为她们看到了：这个健康快乐的男孩子就是文思远！

Key Words 关键词 (Guānjiàncí)

1 玩 (wán) *v.* to play

2 理 (lǐ) *v.* to pay attention to

3 好像 (hǎoxiàng) *v.* it seems

4 阿姨 (āyí) *n.* maid, housekeeper

5 开心 (kāixīn) *adj.* happy

6 看起来 (kànqǐlai) *vc.* to look (a certain way)

7 瘦 (shòu) *adj.* thin

8 生病 (shēngbìng) *v.* to get sick

9 总是 (zǒngshì) *adv.* always

10 生气 (shēngqì) *vo.* to get angry

11 哭 (kū) *v.* to cry

12 为了 (wèile) *conj.* for the purpose of, in order to

13 听话 (tīnghuà) *vo.* to obey, *lit.* "to listen to (someone's) words"

14 关心 (guānxīn) *v.* to be concerned about

15 平时 (píngshí) *tn.* usual; usually

16 一定 (yīdìng) *adv.* definitely

17 出事 (chūshì) *vo.* to have an accident

18 后来 (hòulái) *tn.* afterwards

19 难过 (nánguò) *adj.* to feel upset

20 发现 (fāxiàn) *v.* to discover

21 家人 (jiārén) *n.* family

22 叔叔 (shūshu) *n.* uncle, father's younger brother

23 带 (dài) *v.* to bring

24 应该 (yīnggāi) *aux.* should, ought to

25 奇怪 (qíguài) *adj.* weird, strange

26 里面 (lǐmiàn) *n.* inside

27 有意思 (yǒuyìsi) *adj.* interesting

28 想法 (xiǎngfǎ) *n.* thinking, idea

29 草地 (cǎodì) *n.* lawn, grassy area

30 记住 (jìzhu) *vc.* to remember, to memorize

31 衣服 (yīfu) *n.* clothing

32 健康 (jiànkāng) *adj.* healthy

33 一直 (yīzhí) *adv.* all along

34 学会 (xuéhuì) *vc.* to learn

35 往前 (wǎngqián) *phr.* forward

36 样子 (yàngzi) *n.* appearance

37 种 (zhòng) *v.* to plant (a tree or other plant)

38 不怎么 (bùzěnme) *adv.* not very

39 做事 (zuòshì) *vo.* to do things

40 墙 (qiáng) *n.* wall

41 忘记 (wàngjì) *v.* to forget

42 打理 (dǎlǐ) *v.* to take care of

43 掉 (diào) *v.* to fall

44 声 (shēng) *n.* noise, sound

45 紧张 (jǐnzhāng) *adj.* nervous

46 记得 (jìde) *v.* to remember

47 试 (shì) *v.* to try

48 打开 (dǎkāi) *vc.* to open

49 方向 (fāngxiàng) *n.* direction

50 不然 (bùrán) *conj.* otherwise

51 树林 (shùlín) *n.* forest

52 小心 (xiǎoxīn) *v.* to be careful

53 亮 (liàng) *adj.* bright

54 钥匙 (yàoshi) *n.* key

55 秘密 (mìmì) *n.* secret

56 关上 (guānshang) *vc.* to close

57 工具 (gōngjù) *n.* tool

58 问题 (wèntí) *n.* problem

59 种子 (zhǒngzi) *n.* seed

60 放心 (fàngxīn) *v.* to relax, to be relieved

61 办法 (bànfǎ) *n.* way, method

62 睡觉 (shuìjiào) *vo.* to sleep

63 家具 (jiājù) *n.* furniture

64 左右 (zuǒyòu) *adv.* about, more or less, *lit.* "left-right"

65 常常 (chángcháng) *adv.* often

66 旅行 (lǚxíng) *v.* to travel

67 恨 (hèn) *v.* to hate

68 起床 (qǐchuáng) *vo.* to get out of bed

69 可能 (kěnéng) *adv.* possibly, maybe

70 走路 (zǒulù) *vo.* to walk

71 轮椅 (lúnyǐ) *n.* wheelchair

72 认真 (rènzhēn) *adj.* serious, earnest

73 有用 (yǒuyòng) *adj.* useful

Part of Speech Key

adj. Adjective

adv. Adverb

aux. Auxiliary Verb

conj. Conjunction

mw. Measure Word

n. Noun

on. Onomatopoeia

part. Particle

pn. Proper Noun

tn. Time Noun

v. Verb

vc. Verb plus Complement

vo. Verb plus Object

Discussion Questions
讨论问题 (Tǎolùn Wèntí)

Chapter 1 没有人喜欢的女孩

1. 李叶是一个什么样的女孩? 为什么没有人喜欢李叶?

2. 你知道海南吗? 海南是什么样的地方?

3. 李叶的妈妈好像一点也不喜欢李叶。你觉得真的有这样的妈妈吗?

Chapter 2 去南京

1. 你知道南京吗? 你觉得南京怎么样?

2. 你喜欢文先生这样的家吗? 为什么?

3. 你觉得文太太死了以后, 文先生有什么变化(biànhuà)?

Chapter 3 这个阿姨不一样

1. 王乐心跟李叶以前的阿姨有什么不一样?

2. 你觉得王乐心的家和李叶的家有什么不一样?

3. 如果王乐心和李叶经常在一起, 你觉得她们会有什么变化(biànhuà)?

4. 你有王乐心这样的朋友吗? 说一说他们是什么样的人。

Chapter 4 有人在哭

1. 林爷爷是一个老人, 你觉得他可以做李叶的朋友吗?

2. 如果你是李叶, 你会用什么办法进秘密花园?

3. 为什么文太太死了以后, 文先生关了秘密花园?

Chapter 5 秘密花园

1. 你觉得是谁在哭? 为什么?

2. 如果你是李叶, 马阿姨总是生气, 你会听她的话吗?

3. 想象一下, 李叶走进秘密花园以后, 看到了一个什么样的花园?

Chapter 6 两个人的秘密

1. 李叶为什么很喜欢王乐天? 王乐天是什么样的人?

2. 李叶为什么会告诉王乐天她找到了秘密花园的钥匙?

3. 如果你是李叶, 你会告诉王乐天花园的秘密吗? 为什么?

Chapter 7 是他在哭!

1. 你会和文思远这样的人做朋友吗? 为什么?

2. 文先生为什么很少去看文思远?

3. 你觉得李叶应该让文思远知道秘密花园的事吗? 为什么?

Chapter 8 三个人的秘密

1. 认识李叶以后, 文思远有了什么变化(biànhuà)?

2. 如果你是李叶, 看到文思远那么生气, 你会怎么做?

Chapter 9 一起去花园

1. 文思远是怎么不让别人知道他们的秘密的?

2. 你觉得秘密花园会让文思远发生什么变化?

Chapter 10 你可以做到!

1. 现在的花园有了什么变化?

2. 如果你是林爷爷, 看到三个孩子在秘密花园里, 你会怎么做?

3. 文思远为什么要站起来?

Chapter 11 在花园里!

1. 文思远为什么不让别人发现他比以前健康了?

2. 秘密花园让文思远和李叶学会了什么?

Chapter 12 没有秘密了

1. 如果你是文思远, 看到文先生的时候, 你会说什么?

2. 文先生看到现在的秘密花园以后, 他的想法有什么变化?

Appendix A:
Character Comparison Reference

This appendix is designed to help Chinese teachers and learners use the Mandarin Companion Graded Readers as a companion to the most popular university textbooks and the HSK word lists.

The tables below compare the characters and vocabulary used in other study materials with those found in this Mandarin Companion graded reader. The tables below will display the exact characters and vocabulary used in this book and not covered by these sources. A learner who has studied these textbooks will likely find it easier to read this graded reader by focusing on these characters and words.

Integrated Chinese Level 1, Part 1-2 (3rd Ed.)

Words and characters in this story not covered by these two textbooks:

Character	Pinyin	Word(s)	Pinyin
叶	yè	李叶 叶子 树叶	Lǐ Yè yèzi shùyè
密	mì	秘密	mìmì
秘	mì	秘密	mìmì
鸟	niǎo	鸟	niǎo
声	shēng	哭声 关门声 大声 小声 叫声 风声 笑声	kūshēng guānmén shēng dàshēng xiǎoshēng jiàoshēng fēngshēng xiàoshēng
门	mén	门 出门 关门 开门 打开门	mén chūmén guānmén kāimén dǎkāi mén

Character	Pinyin	Word(s)	Pinyin
树	shù	树 种树 树叶 树上 树林 树下	shù zhòngshù shùyè shù shang shùlín shù xia
草	cǎo	草 草地 种草 绿草	cǎo cǎodì zhòng cǎo lǜcǎo
奇	qí	奇怪	qíguài
怪	guài	奇怪	qíguài
林	lín	树林 林爷爷	shùlín Lín yéye
钥	yào	钥匙	yàoshi
匙	shi	钥匙	yàoshi
总	zǒng	总是	zǒngshì
轮	lún	轮椅	lúnyǐ
风	fēng	风 风声	fēng fēngshēng
墙	qiáng	墙 墙边	qiáng qiáng biān
掉	diào	掉下来	diào xiàlai
恨	hèn	恨	hèn
向	xiàng	方向	fāngxiàng

New Practical Chinese Reader, Books 1-2 (1st Ed.)

Words and characters in this story not covered by these two textbooks:

Character	Pinyin	Word(s)	Pinyin
叶	yè	李叶 叶子 树叶	Lǐ Yè yèzi shùyè
姨	yí	阿姨	āyí
密	mì	秘密	mìmì
秘	mì	秘密	mìmì
叔	shū	叔叔	shūshu
鸟	niǎo	鸟	niǎo
草	cǎo	草 草地 种草 绿草	cǎo cǎodì zhòng cǎo lùcǎo
奇	qí	奇怪	qíguài
怪	guài	奇怪	qíguài
健	jiàn	健康	jiànkāng
康	kāng	健康	jiànkāng
直	zhí	一直	yīzhí
紧	jǐn	紧张	jǐnzhāng
轮	lún	轮椅	lúnyǐ
椅	yǐ	轮椅	lúnyǐ
更	gèng	更	gèng
黄	huáng	黄色	huángsè
墙	qiáng	墙 墙边	qiáng qiáng biān
具	jù	工具	gōngjù
近	jìn	近	jìn
恨	hèn	恨	hèn

Hanyu Shuiping Kaoshi (HSK) Levels 1-3

Words and characters in this story not covered by these three levels:

Character	Pinyin	Word(s)	Pinyin
叶	yè	李叶 叶子 树叶	Lǐ Yè yèzi shùyè
王	wáng	王乐心 王乐天	Wáng Lèxīn Wáng Lètiān
密	mì	秘密	mìmì
秘	mì	秘密	mìmì
知	zhī	知道	zhīdao
从	cóng	从来没有 从来不 从那以后 从	cónglái méiyǒu cónglái bù cóng nà yǐhòu cóng
像	xiàng	像 好像	xiàng hǎoxiàng
死	sǐ	死	sǐ
林	lín	树林 林爷爷	shùlín Lín yéye
紧	jǐn	紧张	jǐnzhāng
轮	lún	轮椅	lúnyǐ
更	gèng	更	gèng
海	hǎi	海南	Hǎinán
墙	qiáng	墙 墙边	qiáng qiáng biān
具	jù	工具	gōngjù
往	wǎng	往	wǎng
掉	diào	掉下来	diào xiàlai
恨	hèn	恨	hèn

Appendix B: Grammar Point Index

For learners new to reading in Chinese, an understanding of grammar points can be extremely helpful for learners and teachers. The following is a list of the most challenging grammar points used in this graded reader.

These grammar points correspond to the Common European Framework of Reference for Languages (CEFR) level A2 or above. The full list with explanations and examples of each grammar point can be found on the Chinese Grammar Wiki, the internet's definitive source of information on Chinese grammar.

CHAPTER 1	
Modifying nouns with phrase + "de"	[Phrase] + 的 + Noun
Measure words for counting	Number + MW + Noun
"Not very" with "bu tai"	不太 + Adj
Modifying nouns with adjective + "de"	Adj + 的 + Noun
"Zai" following verbs	Verb + 在 + Place
The "zui" superlative	最 + Adj
Pronoun "mei" for "every"	每 + MW (+ Noun)
Expressing "every" with "mei" and "dou"	每 + MW + Noun + 都 + Adj/Verb
Expressing "and" with "he"	N1 + 和 + N2
Expressing "together" with "yiqi"	一起 + V
The "all" adverb	都 + Verb / 都 + Adj
Expressing "in addition" with "haiyou"	Clause 1 ， 还有 + (,)+ Clause 2
"It seems" with "haoxiang"	好像……
"Not at all"	一点(儿) 也 不……
"If…, then…" with "ruguo…, jiu…"	如果……，就……
Causative verbs	Noun1 + 让/叫/请 + Noun2……
Result complements "dao" and "jian"	Verb + 到 / 见
Measure words to differentiate	这 / 那 + MW (+ N)
Expressing ability or possibility	能 + V
"Both A and B" with "you"	又…… 又……
Expressing "and also" with "hai"	还 + Verb

"Always" with "zongshi"	总是 + Verb
At the time when	……的时候
Auxiliary verb "hui" for "will"	会 + Verb
Special verbs with "hen"	很 + Verb
Referring to "all" using "suoyou"	所有… 都…
"Never" with "conglai"	从来不 / 从来没(有)
Expressing experiences with "guo"	Verb + 过
Comparing specifically with "xiang"	Noun1 + 像 + Noun2 + (那么……)
Explaining results with "suoyi"	……，所以…
Expressing purpose with "weile"	为了 + Purpose + Verb
Expressing "as one likes" with "jiu"	还 + Verb / Adj
Continuation with "hai"	还 + Verb / Adj
Again in the past with "you"	又 + Verb
Explaining causes with "yinwei"	Result, 因为 + Reason
"Would like to" with "xiang"	想 + Verb
Wanting to do something with "yao"	要 + Verb
"Before" in general	以前 + Subject + Verb + Object
"Even more" with "geng"	更 + Adj
Expressing "with" with "gen"	跟…… + Verb
Change of state with "le"	……了
Expressing lateness with "cai"	才
Emphasizing quantity with "dou"	大家 / 很多人 + 都……
Expressing earliness with "jiu"	就
Expressing completion with "le"	Subject + Verb + 了 + Object
Complements with "dao", "gei" and "zai"	Verb + 到 / 给 / 在……
Expressing duration with "le"	Verb + 了 + Duration
Sequencing past events with "houlai"	……，后来……
Using "ji" to mean "several"	Subj. + 在 + Place + V
CHAPTER 2	
After a specific time	Time/Time phrase + 以后
Two words for "but"	Statement, 可是/但是 + [transitional statement]
"Yinggai" for should	应该 / 该 + Verb
Adjs with "name" and "zheme"	那么 / 这么 + Adj

Yes-no questions with "ma"	...吗?
Modifying nouns with phrase + "de"	(Phrase) + 的 + N
"Already" with "yijing"	已经……了
Aspect particle "zhe"	Verb + 着
Expressing permission	可以 + V
Basic comparisons with "yiyang"	Noun1 + 跟 + Noun2 + 一样 + Adj
Before a specific time	Time / Verb + 以前
Negative commands with "bie"	别 + Verb
CHAPTER 3	
Positive and negative potential complements	Verb + 得 / 不……
Expressing "a little too" with "you dian"	有点(儿) + Adj
Using "dui"	对 + Noun……
Using "zai" with verbs	Subj. + 在 + Place + Verb
Ordinal numbers with "di"	第 + Number (+ MW)
"Just" with "gang"	Subject + 刚 + V.
Expressing "a bit too"	Adj + (一) 点儿
Verbing briefly	Verb + 一下
"Some" using "yixie"	一些 + Noun
Verbs with "gei"	Subject + 给 + Target + Verb +
Expressing a learned skill	Subject + 会 + Verb + Object
Simultaneous tasks with "yibian"	(一)边 + V, (一)边 + Verb
Suggestions with "ba"	……吧
Expressing location with "zai...shang/xia/li"	在 + Location + 上/下/里/旁边
"Shi... de" construction	是…… 的
Turning adjectives into adverbs	Adj + 地 + Verb
Measure words for verbs	Verb + Number + MW
"-wan" result complement	Subject + Verb + 完 + Object
Verb reduplication with "yi"	Verb + 一 + Verb
Comparing "chao" "xiang" and "wang"	朝 vs 向 vs 往
CHAPTER 4	
Expressing actions in progress	(正)在 + Verb
Reduplication of adjectives	Adj + Adj

Softening speech with "ba"	……吧。
"Not very" with "bu zenme"	不怎么 + Adj
Adding emphasis with "jiushi"	就是
Indicating a number in excess	Number + 多
Appearance with "kanqilai"	看起来……
Basic comparisons with "bi"	Noun1 + 比 + Noun2 + Adj
Negative commands with "bu yao"	不要 + Verb
Direction complement	Verb (+ Direction) + 来 / 去
Questions with "le ma"	Verb + 了 + 吗?
Result complement "-cuo"	Verb + 错
CHAPTER 5	
Expressing "excessively" with "tai"	太 + Adj + 了
"De" (modal particle)	……的
Expressing "otherwise" with "yaobu"	要不……
CHAPTER 6	
Verbs with "gei"	Subject + 给 + Target + Verb + Object
CHAPTER 7	
About to happen with "kuai... le"	快 + Verb/Verb Phrase + 了
Intensifying with "duo"	Subject + 多 + Adj !
CHAPTER 8	
"As long as" with "zhiyao"	只要……，就……
Expressing duration (ongoing)	Verb + 了 + Duration + 了
"Never again" with "zai ye bu"	再也不 + Verb
CHAPTER 9	
Expressing purpose with "weile"	为了 + Purpose + Verb
Mistakenly think that	以为……
Expressing duration of inaction	Subject + Duration + 没 + Verb + Object + 了
CHAPTER 10	
Asking why with "zenme"	怎么……?
CHAPTER 11	
There are no new grammar points in this chapter.	
CHAPTER 12	
Softening the tone of questions with "ne"	……呢?

Credits

Original Author: Frances Hodgson Burnett

Series Editor: John Pasden

Lead Writer: Yang Renjun

Content Editor: Yu Cui

Proofreader: Zhang Pei

Illustrator: Hu Shen

Producer: Jared Turner

Acknowledgments

Thank you to Yang Renjun, Yu Cui, Song Shen and the entire team at AllSet Learning for working on this project and contributing the perfect mix of talent to produce this series.

Thank you to Mark Neville who tested this book with students in his Chinese class and offered valuable insights and edits. We're grateful to Dong Hua and Zhang Pei for academic feedback, and to our enthusiastic testers Erick Garcia, Ben Slye, Brandon Sanchez, and Mary Ann Abejuro.

A special thanks to Rob Waring to whom we refer to as the "godfather of extensive reading" for his encouragement, expert advice, and support with this project.

Thank you to Heather Turner for being the inspiration behind the entire series and never wavering in her belief. Thank you to Song Shen for supporting us, handling all the small thankless tasks, and spurring us forward if we dared to fall behind.

Moreover, we will be forever grateful for Yuehua Liu and Chengzhi Chu for pioneering the first graded readers in Chinese and to whom we owe a debt of gratitude for their years of tireless work to bring these type of materials to the Chinese learning community.

About Mandarin Companion

Mandarin Companion was started by Jared Turner and John Pasden who met one fateful day on a bus in Shanghai when the only remaining seat left them sitting next to each other. A year later, Jared had greatly improved his Chinese using extensive reading but was frustrated at the lack of suitable reading materials. He approached John with the prospect of creating their own series. Having worked in Chinese education for nearly a decade, John was intrigued with the idea and thus began the Mandarin Companion series.

John majored in Japanese in college, but started learning Mandarin and later moved to China where his learning accelerated. After developing language proficiency, he was admitted into an all-Chinese masters program in applied linguistics at East China Normal University in Shanghai. Throughout his learning process, John developed an open mind to different learning styles and a tendency to challenge conventional wisdom in the field of teaching Chinese. He has since worked at ChinesePod as academic director and host, and opened his own consultancy, AllSet Learning, in Shanghai to help individuals acquire Chinese language proficiency. He lives in Shanghai with his wife and children.

After graduate school and with no Chinese language skills, Jared decided to move to China with his young family in search of career opportunities. Later while working on an investment project, Jared learned about extensive reading and decided that if it was as effective as it claimed to be, it could help him learn Chinese. In three months, he read 10 Chinese graded readers and his language ability quickly improved from speaking words and phrases to a conversational level. Jared has an MBA from Purdue University and a bachelor in Economics from the University of Utah. He lives in Shanghai with his wife and children.

Other Stories from Mandarin Companion

Level 1 Readers: 300 Characters

The Monkey's Paw《猴爪》
by W.W. Jacobs

Mr. and Mrs. Zhang live with their grown son Guisheng who works at a factory. One day Mr. Qian, an old friend of Mr. Zhang, comes to visit the family after having spent years traveling in the mysterious hills of China's Yunnan Province. Mr. Qian tells the Zhang family of a monkey's paw he was given that has magical powers to grant three wishes to the holder. Against his better judgement, Mr. Qian reluctantly gives the monkey paw to the Zhang family, along with a warning that the wishes come with a great price for trying to change ones fate…

The Sixty-Year Dream 《六十年的梦》
based on "Rip Van Winkle" by Washington Irving

Zhou Xuefa (Rip Van Winkle) is well loved by everyone in his town, everyone except his nagging wife. With his faithful dog Blackie, Zhou Xuefa spends his time playing with kids, helping neighbors, and discussing politics in the teahouse. One day after a bad scolding from his wife, he goes for a walk into the mountains and meets a mysterious old man who appears to be from an ancient time. The man invites him into his mountain home for a meal and after drinking some wine, Zhou Xuefa falls into a deep sleep. He awakes to a time very different than what he once knew.

The Country of the Blind 《盲人国》
by H.G. Wells

"In the country of the blind, the one-eyed man is king," repeats in Chen Fangyuan's mind after he finds himself trapped in a valley holding a community of people for whom a disease eliminated their vision many generations before and no longer have a concept of sight. Chen Fangyuan quickly finds that these people have developed their other senses to compensate for their lack of sight. His insistence that he can see causes the entire community to believe he is crazy. With no way out, Chen Fangyuan begins to accept his fate until one day the village doctors believe they now understand what is the cause of his insanity... those useless round objects in his eye sockets.

Sherlock Holmes and the Curly Haired Company
《卷发公司的案子》
based on "Sherlock Holmes and the Case of the Red Headed League" by Sir Arthur Conan Doyle

Mr. Xie was recently hired by the Curly Haired Company. For a significant weekly allowance, he was required to sit in an office and copy articles from a book, while in the meantime his assistant looked after his shop. He had answered an advertisement in the paper and although hundreds of people applied, he was the only one selected because of his very curly hair. When the company unexpectedly closes, Mr. Xie visits Gao Ming (Sherlock Holmes) with his strange story. Gao Ming is certain something is not right, but will he solve the mystery in time?

Mandarin companion is producing a growing library of graded readers for Chinese language learners.

Visit our website for the newest books available:

www.MandarinCompanion.com

CPSIA information can be obtained
at www.ICGtesting.com
Printed in the USA
LVOW05s1120281216
518934LV00003B/73/P